Noah's Scrapbook

Noah's Scrapbook

by

Joan Last

with illustrations by
Angus James

The Pentland Press
Edinburgh – Cambridge – Durham – USA

© Joan Last, 2000

First published in 2000 by
The Pentland Press Ltd
1 Hutton Close,
South Church
Bishop Auckland
Durham

All rights reserved
Unauthorised duplication
contravenes existing laws

ISBN 1-85821-830-6

Typeset by Carnegie Publishing, Carnegie House, Chatsworth Road, Lancaster
Printed and bound by Antony Rowe

For Charlotte and William

About the author

Joan Last O.B.E has been writing poetry since childhood, but only as a hobby. As a musician she has had a distinguished career, first as a pianist and then, after an accident to her hand, as a teacher, author and composer of piano music. She has written three books on piano teaching and interpretation which were given rave reviews and have been translated into several languages and sell world-wide. As a professor at the Royal Academy of Music she received their highest award, the Hon. R.A.M. She has been an examiner and adjudicator and has travelled the world giving piano seminars and master classes in fourteen different countries, returning by popular request over and over again. Her appearance at New York's Carnegie Hall was an unqualified success. She has also worked at music camps as far afield as the Rocky Mountains. Her musical works in print number over one hundred, with more in the pipeline. She was awarded the O.B.E in 1988 for services to music education. Now semi-retired, she has returned to her love of writing poetry and this collection is the result.

Contents

Noah's Ark	1
The Panda	2
The Centipede	3
Bats	4
Dolphins	5
The Robin	6
The Bluetit	7
Toad Hall Revisited	8
The Gnu	10
The Elephant and the Bumblebee	11
The Intrepid Penguin	12
The Owl and the Pussycat	14
Gilbert the Giraffe	16
The Industrious Beaver	18
The Hummingbird	20
The Errant Pigeon	22
The Grand Old Buffel	24
The Disobedient Monkey	26
The Handsome Warthog	28
The Kangabird	29
Rabbits	30
Two of a Kind	32
The Astronaut Ape	34
The Polar Bear	35
The Flea and the Fly	36
The Whale and his Wife	37
A Family Tragedy	39

The Uninvited Guest	40
Hospital in British Columbia	41
The Sheep and the Goat	42
The Intimidating Serpent	43
The Mongoose	44
Man's Best Friend	45
The Condescending Cat	46
The Trendy Squirrels	48
A Tragic Flight	50
Sports Day	52
Tiger Blues	54
The Exemplary Canary	55
Cow Cantata	56
The Porcupines	57
Eisteddfod	58
Ship of the Desert	60
That Horrible Laugh	62
The Stupid Crocodile	63
Lost Property	64
Home at Last	65
Pussycat Paganini	66
The Lion King	67
The Exemplary Cheetah	68
Cooking Instructions	69
Jeremy Fisher	70
Mrs Tiggywinkle	72
The Lazy Sow	74
Time for a Change	76

Noah's Ark

We ought to be thankful to Noah and his wife
　　whose Ark saved the future of Animal Life.
The first Conservationists, do not forget,
　　To whom we all owe a considerable debt.
And though, at the time, it was rather a squash
　　with nowhere to sit or to walk or to wash,
One thing is certain, of this I am sure,
　　More of them came out than went in before.

The Panda

A Panda came from China to live in London Zoo,
   She didn't really like it, with no one there she knew.
The only things she cared for were Bamboo shoots to eat,
   She turned her nose up firmly at vegetables and meat.
They brought another Panda to be her friend and mate,
She didn't like him either and wouldn't make a date.

Yet everybody loves her, with her coat of black and white,
   It's sad she feels so lonely, it doesn't seem quite right.
For her picture has been chosen, to show how great the need
   For Wildlife Conservation, to perpetuate her breed.

The Centipede

The Centipede
   He does not need
to count, like other men,
   He simply waves his legs about
and multiplies by ten.
   He would not choose
A pair of shoes,
   That would not do at all,
He goes to the nearest shop
   And says: 'I'll have them all'.

Bats

Bats are funny little things
   Little furry mice with wings.
They prefer to fly at night
   And give some people quite a fright.
'Bats in the belfry', it is said
   means a rather muddled head.
As for me, I find them fun
   When the daylight hours are done.

Dolphins

A Dolphin and Dolphinet
  are man and wife, so not forget!
Their cleverness is much abused
  For show and tricks they're often used.
They should be free to swim the sea
  And live their lives out happily.

The Robin

The Robin stays through winter days
   To cheer us with his winning ways.
His red breast acts as timely cheer
   When the frost and cold is here.
He's not afraid of man at all
   And watches from the garden wall
for us to give him tasty fare.
   To let him starve we would not dare!

The Bluetit

I love to watch the bluetit
   coming from his nest,
He enters through a tiny hole
   Where chicks are safe to rest.
We put out nuts and scraps of fat
   For they're his choicest fare,
And, if we're lucky, we may see
   Two bluetits feeding there.

Toad Hall Revisited

Mr Toad, the one you know,
Who stole and drove a car,
Decided he would take up golf
And play a round in par.

He teed his ball at number one
And hit with all his might,
He shouted 'Fore, now what's the score?'
But not a ball in sight.

For Mr Mole, of years gone by,
had popped up from the ground,
He said: 'Look Toady, what you've done
You've gone and spoilt your round:

Your ball is in my little house,
You'd better come down here
And drink a toast to days gone by,
In half a pint of beer'.

Then Ratty came and Badger too
They said: 'Hullo old chap
'Tis many a day since Kenneth G
Put us on the map.

Look Toady, just a round of golf
a thousand people play,
Why worry, when your name has been
Immortalised this way?'. (*With apologies to Kenneth Grahame*)

The Gnu

The Gnu
In the Zoo,
Was very upset.
So bad, he was visited
by the vet.
The vet's diagnosis
was chronic neurosis
About his name.

He said:
'It's a shame
And who is to blame
For calling him that?

The children can all spell
'Dog' and 'Cat'
And three letter animals
'Cow' 'Pig' or 'Rat';

But they never learn Gnu
Just G N U
No wonder, poor fellow,
He's feeling blue.'

The Elephant and the Bumblebee

Two good friends went out to sea,
An Elephant and a Bumblebee
And when, at last, he sighted land
The Elephant said: 'This is grand!
The only thing that worries me,
I seem to have lost the Bumblebee.'

The Intrepid Penguin

A Penguin decided he'd like to explore
   So he left all his family down by the shore
But he wandered so far that he quite lost his way
   And feared he would never get home that day.

He knocked on the door of a large hotel,
   The Manager, seeing him called out: 'Well
we wanted a waiter and look who's here
   Come in, little man, you have nothing to fear!

'Your coat is just perfect, smart black and white,
   We welcome you here with the greatest delight
The pay is two pounds, but I'll make it three
   For I don't have to buy you a suit, you see!'

The poor little Penguin was given a tray
   And marched to the dining room straight away.
The guests simply loved him, they had to agree
   They'd not seen a waiter as smart as he.

He knew he was trapped, but he kept his head,
   And played out his part until time for bed,
And then, when he knew they were fast asleep,
   Slowly downstairs he began to creep.

He opened a window and, silently,
 slid to the ground, and at last he was free.
And, when he reached home, he declared: Never more
 Must curious Penguins go out and explore!'

The Owl and the Pussycat

The Owl and the Pussycat went to sea
   Many long years ago.
They sailed away, for a year and a day
   To the land where the bong trees grow.
A piggy was willing to sell for a shilling
   The ring on the end of his nose.
They took it away and were married next day
   The Owl had no need to propose.
The Turkey, who lived at the top of a hill,
   With Prayer book, cassock and stole,
Declared they were wed: 'I'll not charge you' he said
   Which was kind, for he lived on the dole.

But nobody tells us what happened next
   We would, all of us, like to know.
     Did they live on an island for twenty years
       In a state of domestic bliss?
Did Pussy purr as he stroked her fur
   And gave her a Goodnight kiss?
     Did he sing her a song as he played his guitar
       And was it a lullaby?
Did he wish her sweet dreams as the evening star
   rose up in a velvet sky?

The Owl, I have heard, is a very wise bird
  And no one would question his brain,
But we would like to know, all those years long ago
  If he brought Pussy home again.
                    With apologies to Edward Lear.

Gilbert the Giraffe

Gilbert, the Giraffe, was very tall
He even made his father look quite small,
    He could reach the highest trees
      and nibble them with ease,
But Gilbert wasn't happy, not at all.

For Gilbert, the Giraffe, was so short-sighted
His early life was permanently blighted:
    He couldn't see his feet
      Which, in fact, were small and neat
So of running he was really quite affrighted.

His mother, who was naturally upset,
took Gilbert to the best Ophthalmic Vet:
    And now, upon his nose,
      Natty spectacles repose
But no one laughs, it isn't etiquette!

Now Gilbert is as happy as can be,
His troubles over now that he can see,
    And all the girls make passes
      At Gilbert in his glasses
With his air of haughty aristocracy.

The Industrious Beaver

The Beaver is a builder
    Superior to man,
No one had to teach him
    how to build a river dam.

He bites through wood with greatest ease,
    He chooses it from fallen trees
And then he drags a branch away
    Makes many journeys in a day.

He shapes a channel for his swim
    And, if you watch, you'll witness him
Carrying his heavy loads
    To where the river swiftly flows.

His wife is waiting at the end
    She twists the branches, makes them bend,
Shapes them in a clever way
    To hold the river's tide at bay.

One day there was a tragedy,
    A really bad emergency,
The dam gave way, the water flowed
    She could not stem the heavy load.

Her husband, he had gone away,
    For her it was a dreadful day.
But Beavers, all along the line,
    came to her aid and just in time:

The dam, once more, was holding fast.
    Her husband came back home at last.
He was, he said, quite horrified
    He'd not been there to stem the tide.

He swam along the river banks
    To give his kindly neighbours thanks.
He promised he'd stay nearer home
    And, no more, far away would roam.

The Hummingbird

One can't describe in just one word
   The clever little Hummingbird,
Performing with amazing skill
   Assisted by his lengthy bill.

Wings beat a thousand times a minute,
   seeks a flower with nectar in it,
Probing, whilst he takes his fill
   With that long and useful bill.

Other birds are not quite sure
   what this hovering act is for.
'He can do it, why can't we?'
   Maybe it is jealousy.

Little bird, he doesn't care,
   Darting swiftly here and there.
Nectar-filled, he flies away.
   He'll be back another day.

The Errant Pigeon

A Pigeon flew a letter from Manchester to Rome:
   There should have been an answer
      But he never came back home.
The owner, duly worried, sent a letter to the Pope
   He thought a man so kindly
      Could offer his some hope.

'Your Holiness, I beg you, give me some advice'.
   The Pope replied: 'A *Pigeon*?
      Two Lira is my price?'

The owner sent the money and awaited a reply
   The Pope wrote: 'In St Peter's Square
      a thousand Pigeons fly,
Just look around Trafalgar and detect a single bird,
   The Square is full of pigeons, the idea is absurd.
It seems to me your Pigeon has found a lady friend,
   I fear he's lost for ever, the search is at an end!'

And so another Pigeon flew from Manchester to Rome,
   Not one, not two, but twenty
      And they never came back home.
The owner sold his pigeons and booked a two way flight.
   He always gets his answers,
      So now it's quite all right.

The Grand Old Buffel

A very old Buffel went into a huffel,
  The reason I wanted to know:
He said: 'Can't you see it's an insult to me?
  I am really a fine Buffalo,
My horns may be breaking, my legs sometimes shaking,
  I'm older than all in the herd,
But, when there's a meeting, I get such a greeting,
  In voting I have the last word!

I once was a danger, a dog in the manger
  But now I'm as calm as can be,
But now take my word, if a Buffalo herd
  comes along: 'Just you shin up a tree,
They really are cruel, don't wait for a duel,
  Get out while the going is good,
Or else, one fine day, I am sorry to say,
  You will end up as Buffalo food'.

NB: Buffel is the Afrikaans for 'Buffalo'.

The Disobedient Monkey

A Monkey, climbing a Mangrove tree,
   Lost his footing and fell in the sea.
He shouted: 'Help' for he could not float,
   So his family borrowed a rowing boat.

And when, at last, they fished him out
   His Grandfather said: 'I rather doubt
we have come in time, I fear he is dead'.
   His Mother said: 'Nonsense! he just needs his bed!'

By happy chance, when they reached dry land,
   a lifeguard offered to lend a hand.
He knew what to do and he did it quick
   So the poor little Monkey was rather sick.

Before very long he was right as rain
   And his Mother said: 'Never do *that* again'.
But the very next day that little Monkee
   Lost his footing and fell in the sea.

This time no one else was around
So, sadly, the poor little Monkey was drowned.

The Handsome Warthog

Whoever gave the Warthog
   such an unbecoming name?
He may be rather ugly,
   But still, it seems a shame.
He is the best of Fathers
   All the children love their Dad.
And, as for Mrs Warthog
   She thinks he's quite the lad.
He trots along so smartly
   His tail up in the air.
Perhaps we need not worry,
   It seems he doesn't care.
It's obvious that really
   He's a happy little man.
He's always been a Warthog
   Ever since his breed began.

The Kangabird

A Kangaroo didn't care for the Zoo
   And so he decided to quit, wouldn't you?
He practised leaping hour after hour
   Till he reached as high as the Post Office tower,
Then one fine evening, after dark,
   he landed lightly in Regents Park.

A Kangaroo has escaped from the Zoo!
   What a commotion, what a to-do,
Police blew whistles, traffic stopped
   And out of the window heads all popped:
But our little friend had leapt so high
   The search was continued in the sky.

What happened next I cannot tell
   For nobody knows what really befell,
But, way down under, it *has* been heard
   That someone has sighted a KANGABIRD!

Rabbits

Rabbits, they have habits as everybody knows,
They rear a lot of babies then stand them all in rows.
   The eldest son is Peter,
   The youngest Twinkletoes.

Their father gives a lesson how a rabbit's life is run,
They may play around all evening,
Unless they hear a gun,
   Then, quickly, they must scamper
     to the burrow safe and well;
   He speaks of Uncle Ronnie,
     A sorry tale to tell.

   But Peter said: 'I'll show 'em
   I'll go out for a dare!'
So out he ran, a gun went *bang* and Peter had a scare,
His Mother said: 'Now Peter, you know what *not* to do
   And what your father told you
     Is absolutely true.'

Two of a Kind

A Horse met a Zebra one fine night:
'My goodness' he said: 'You gave me a fright,
   You look like a horse
   But I must say, of course,
That I never saw one who looked quite such a sight.

'There are cream horses, black horses, chestnut and grey
   Piebald and skewbald, but none I must say
who looks quite like you, or can it be true
   That black and white stirpes are in vogue today?'

The Zebra replied, with a haughty stare:
   'It may seem to you I am rather rare
But, in Africa's plains, the Zebra reigns
   Untroubled by man and free as air'.

'No one on my back will ever sit
   I never would tolerate bridle and bit,
I'd hate to run races and measure my paces
   If put in a stable I'd certainly quit.

And so, my dear friend, you must surely agree
   What is right for you isn't right for me
And, though it is stated we're closely related
   You're servile to man whilst I roam wild and free.'

The Astronaut Ape

A clever Baboon built a fine Space Balloon
Determined, he stated, to visit the moon,
   His wife was upset: 'Please don't leave me, my pet,
   I don't want to lose my dear husband just yet'.

But he set off next day on the fourteenth of May
And no one had tracked him by June.
   So now a new race carries on up in space
   To find the Baboon who set off for the moon.

It may be a record, but no one yet knows
If this difficult project successfully goes.
   But, if that Baboon really reaches the moon,
   A record is made
      That will put in the shade
      The achievements of man
      Since space travel began.

But one thing is sure
   Man will go up once more
And visit new planets
   To come to the fore
of that Cheeky Baboon
   Who set off for the moon,
They'll break up *his* record
   And do it quite soon.

The Polar Bear

The Polar bear has lived on earth a thousand years or more
He's larger than he was at first, but no one knows for sure.
    Worshipped by the vikings eight centuries ago
      And used as gifts for royalty, as history tells us so.
He seeks for seal holes in the ice, the seal's a dainty dish
And, failing that, his choice will be a large and luscious fish.
And, though he roams the Arctic, his life is far from free;
    The Eskimos will kill him for food and family.
    The greedy hunters shoot him, his fur is valued high.
The taxidermist stuffs him, Museums to display.
And, worst of all, they trap him to put in Public Zoos
    In such a situation his freedom he will lose.

But now the Conservationists
    have set the Polar free.
Determined to protect him
    With his wife and family.

The Flea and the Fly

A House fly, to his friend the Flea,
    Said: 'Really, you must look at me
For I can drive the humans mad
    And make their choicest meat go bad
Left on the dresser, nice and fresh,
    Covered with a piece of mesh
I know how to crawl inside,
    Take the humans for a ride.
When I've wandered round a bit
    Food, for eating, isn't fit'.

The Flea replied: 'That's *very* good,
    It's right to spoil the humans' food,
For me it is the other way
    I treat the humans as my prey:
I wait till they are fast asleep
    And then, between the sheets, I creep.
I take one bite and that's enough,
    The humans wakes up in a huff,
He scratches hard to no avail
    And that completes *my* little tale'.

    The Fly said: 'Fine I must agree
        You really are as good as me,
    So let's shake hands, my clever Flea,
        To taunt our common enemy.'

The Whale and his Wife

One day, when enjoying an afternoon sail,
   I saw, in the distance, a very large Whale.
It was quite alarming, I'm sure you'll agree
   when he seemed to be making a bee-line for me.
My thoughts turned to Jonah, I hoped to be spared,
   The nearer that Whale came to more I was scared.

But, as it turned out, I had nothing to fear
   He came right alongside and spoke, loud and clear:
'Please, sir, can you tell if it's six o'clock yet?
   My watch isn't going, it got rather wet,
I promised the wife I'd be home quite by six
   And, if I'm late, I will be in a fix.
For then there will be no nice supper for me
   Just a handful of sprats and a cold cup of tea.'

I said: 'Don't you worry, it's not quarter to,'
   And the Whale, he was off like a bolt from the blue.
It seemed quite amazing that, all through his life
   That very large Whale lived in fear of his wife.

A Family Tragedy

A Lion, a Cat and a very small Mouse
   lived, cosy and warm, in a tumble-down house:
     For quite a long time they got on very well
       Till the Cat, feeling hungry one day,
     Disposed of the Mouse in the tumble-down house
   While the Lion was out of the way.
The Lion was angry, the Cat was *his* friend
   And so the Cat came to a miserable end
     And then, feeling rampant, he let out a roar
       That shook the whole house from the roof to the floor.
     Unable to stand all the shaking and strain
   It slowly collapsed in the wind and the rain.
Yet no one is able to understand why
   such good friends be parted
     And, all of them, die.

The Uninvited Guest
(Written in childhood)

My Mummy says we've got a mouse
    She says it's somewhere in the house,
        My Daddy went and bought a trap
A horrid thing that goes off 'SNAP'.
    An Oh, I've hunted everywhere
        To tell the little mouse it's there
I hope he's found another house
    And somewhere where they *want* a mouse.

Hospitality in British Columbia

When climbing in the Rockies
  I saw a big brown bear
    I thought he'd come and grab me
And take me to his lair.
  But not at all, he was, in fact
    a very friendly bear.

He introduced me to his wife,
  And to the cubs as well;
We sat and talked of this and that
  And stocks and shares to sell.

His wife, a kindly lady bear
  Offered me some honey.
    I said: 'How much?'
      She said 'Oh no,
        We don't want any money.'

It was a pleasant afternoon;
  As I went on my way
They said, 'We hope you'll come and stay with us
  Next time you pass this way!'

The Sheep and the Goat

A Sheep and a goat
  went out in a boat
    Though they didn't quite know what for.
Said the Sheep to the Goat:
  'If we don't stay afloat
    We'll both have to swim for the shore'.
Said the Goat to the Sheep:
  'Then a watch you must keep
    For I'm busy now, writing my notes
As to whether they'll think
  If we fall in the drink,
    They can sort out the Sheep from the Goats'.

The Intimidating Serpent

I don't like Snakes, no not at all
  Slimy, wriggly things that crawl,
    I wouldn't wear one round my neck
      I'd soon become a nervous wreck.
        Yet some there are, who do contend
    A Snake is quite a perfect friend.
They keep one of these slimy things
Just as we keep a bird that sings.

The music that they play, to charm
the Snake fills my heart with alarm:
As, from the basket, up her rears
The player says: 'My Snakes are dears.'
And I reply: 'You must be mad
It's only just a stupid fad.'

  I know not everyone agrees
    But Snakes, they seem to make me freeze.
      I would not keep one as a pet
        Not even for a handsome bet.

    And, when the Cobra lifts his head,
  His venom strikes his victim dead
Unless an antidote is found,
  Not likely there is one around.
    And everybody says: 'Dear me,
      How lucky 'twas not you or me.'

The Mongoose

We had a little Mongoose
  to keep the snakes at bay;
We loved our Mongoose very much
  And told him so each day.
      And then, one day, he disappeared
      And for his life we greatly feared.

Had he been taken by a snake
  Who poisoned him for vengeance' sake?
We hunted high, we hunted low,
  We missed our little Mongoose so.

      But, after all, he was not dead
      Just curled up in a flower bed.

Man's Best Friend

Of all animal society dogs excel in their variety:
   Rough hair, smooth hair, coats of silk,
Lap dogs fed on creamy milk,
   Large dogs, small dogs, thin or fat,
      Noses aquiline or flat.
Dogs of highest pedigree
   Boasting of a family tree.
Dogs who work to earn their keep,
   Lead the blind or herd the sheep,
      Help the police to combat crime,
      Run a race in record time.

But the dog so many need
Isn't any special breed,
Doesn't need a pedigree,
Loved by all the family,
Loyal and faithful
To the end,
Known to all as
MAN'S BEST FRIEND ...

The Condescending Cat

The dog is known as 'Man's best friend'
   But Cats, they only condescend
to rub against your legs for food
   Or purr, if they are in the mood.
If Pussy jumps up on your lap
   You feel you are a splendid chap.
'Just look,' you say, 'she's chosen me
   Of all the present company,'

And, though her claws destroy your knees
   You sit quite still, you nearly freeze
For Pussy *mustn't* be upset,
   Just for the moment she's *your* pet.

   I don't mean to malign the cat
      For, whether she is thin or fat,
   And though she has the wish to roam,
      She'll soon be running back for home,
And, entering through her cat-flap,
Will purr again upon you lap.

The Trendy Squirrels

A Squirrel has a bushy tail
   Used as a rudder or a sail:
It guides him up the tallest trees
   And shelters him from winter's freeze
Whoever heard a squirrel sneeze?

He feeds on nuts and pine cones too,
   He chooses them when buds are new,
He nibbles them with tail erect,
   And then some more he must collect
to build a store for winter time
   When trees are thick with frost and rime.

One day he had a big surprise
   He said: 'Can I believe my eyes?
My coat is red, but now I see
   a Squirrel different from me;
It's very odd, his coat is grey
   I wonder what he has to say.'

The grey declared: 'It's very true
   I'm not as elegant as you.
I hope you will be good to me,
   We've much in common you'll agree:
I travelled here from way out west
   Some people say I am a pest.'

Red Squirrel said: 'Oh that's all right
   I have no wish to start a fight
Come now, my friend, let's shake a paw
   We'll talk of differences no more
I'll treat you in a kindly way,
   Invite you to my family drey,
For, after all, it must be said
   Though you are grey and I am red
In other ways we're much the same
   For being grey *you're* not to blame.'

A Tragic Flight

The Ostrich said: 'Why can't I fly?
I'd like to know the reason why,
   I am a bird
   It's quite absurd,
I really think I'll have a try.'

The Emu said: 'The same for me
I should be nesting in a tree,
   I am a bird
   It's quite absurd,
With you, my friend, I do agree.'

   So, hand in hand, they climbed the hill:
Their friends called: 'Stop, you've not the skill
   You're bound to have a dreadful spill.'

They heeded not these words so wise,
   'What nonsense, it's a pack of lies
     We'll show that we can reach the skies
   Because we have the will.'

They stood upon the highest cliff
   From where the wind blew, cold and stiff
     And then they leapt, their friends all wept
   'If only our advice they'd kept.'

A tragedy, that foolish leap
   They landed in a mangled heap,
     Too late, indeed, their fearful screech
        With feathers scattered o'er the beach.

Their friends said: 'Well, we did our best
   They would not notice our request
A burial at sea seems right,
   We'll do it in the fading light'.
They scraped the feathers from the sands
   A nasty job, birds have no hands.
They placed them in a rowing boat
   At sunset they were all afloat.
They said a simple prayer or two,
   It was the best that they could do.
And never, since that fatal day,
   Have birds been tempted in this way.

Sports Day

The Animal Sports day is held once a year
   And everyone comes to take part, or to cheer
First race on the programme, the one hundred metre
   And I, for my money, am backing the Cheetah.

In high jump Impala and Springbok compete,
   To see their high leaping is really a treat.
For long jump my view is the large Kangaroo
   Whilst those of small size will be Wallaby's prize.

The Elephant thrills with his weight lifting skills
   And Monkeys climb trees with the greatest of ease
But that is not all, the winner will be
   the one who gets first to the top of the tree.

The swimmers are varied. Some large and some small.
   Imagine a Crocodile doing the crawl.
A handicap system is put to the test
   And everyone swims just the way he knows best.

The Marathon takes up the whole of the day
   With Zebras and Wildebeest leading the way.
But forty two miles is a long way to go
   And some, who are weaklings, say: 'Not for me, NO.'

Giraffes act as Umpires and mark from on high.
   Their verdict is final, no right to reply.
So why don't you join us next year, when we meet?
   One pound will secure you the very best seat.

Tiger Blues

The Tiger woke up, in the Zoo,
   to find his stripes were turning blue.
The reason is quite clear to me
   His life is just a travesty.

Open Parks and Game Reserves
   are what each animal deserves.
If you were caged up in a Zoo
   Like the Tiger, *you'd* feel blue.

The Exemplary Canary

Polly the Parrot liked carrot
Bertie the Budgie liked fudge
But Chip, the Canary,
was rather more wary
From birdseed and water she just wouldn't budge.

Polly got bad indigestion,
Bertie soon started to swell.
But Chip, the Canary sang all the day long
And proved to the world you have got to be strong
If you want to remain fit and well.

Cow Cantata

They say that Cows are musical and give a better yield
If soothing music greets their ears when coming from the field.
The trouble is they vary so in music that they choose
Some opt for Jazz whilst others like the music of the Blues.

The highbrow ones like Mendelssohn or Beethoven or Strauss:
Mix all these up and you will find there's Bedlam in the house.

The Porcupines

I often think that Porcupines
   can't really like those prickly spines
     Designed for their protection.

There's such an awful lot they miss
   Without a really close up kiss,
     A sign of true affection.

Perhaps they manage nose to nose,
   Whilst clinging tightly toes to toes,
     But still can't have a cuddle.

For if, by chance, they got too near,
   Those prickly spines, I rather fear,
     would get in quite a muddle.

There was a time when man used quills
   For signing documents and wills
     And letters of intention.

But, now that pens come filled with ink
   The Porcupine, I really think,
     Is not a good invention.

Eisteddfod

The Thrush said to the Nightingale
  'Can it be really true
Some say you have the finest voice?
  On this I challenge you?'
    The Nightingale replied; 'It's clear
     a Judge must be called in
    And he'll compare my lovely voice
     With your appalling din.
  We'll ask the Owl, he's very wise
    He'll say your voice is shrill.'
  The Thrush replied: 'Just wait and see,
    I phrase my notes with skill ... '

        The other birds, on hearing this
          decided to compete:
        The Chaffinch, like a peal of bells
          The Blackbird, soft and sweet.
        The Robin, with his cheerful note
          that captivates the ear.

The Cuckoo, whose distinctive call
  Rings out so loud and clear.
    The Warblers and the Woodpecker
      A 'Waffle' not a song.
        The Sparrows, who, I have to say,
          Should not have come along.

The Judge sat down and listened hard
    to every singing bird
And then he said: 'I cannot tell
    I cannot give my word;
There is so much that I admire
    In every single note,
So I declare a prize for all
    And that's my final vote.

Ship of the Desert

I wonder why the Camel
   deigns to work at all.
He sits, with head held in the air,
   Surveying, with a haughty stare,
Mankind, so weak and small.

His look is so superior
   It makes me feel inferior
And, maybe, that is true.
   We cannot cross the desert sands
And carry folk to far off lands:
   It's something we can't do.

He even joined the Army
   to form the 'Camel Corps'.
I hope he doesn't go on strike
   I couldn't make it on a bike
Or car, and that's for sure.

Perhaps he found life boring
   Before man came along;
And now he'd named 'The Desert Ship',
He's proud to do the longest trip
To prove he's mighty strong.
How strange it is 'the desert ship'
   is plain for all to see,
Yet, you'll never hear a liner called
   'A camel of the Sea'.

That Horrible Laugh

If you have seen a spotted Hyena
  You would hardly believe he could laugh.
He's an ugly beast, to say the least,
  And would never indulge in a chaff.

So if, on Safari, you wake in the night
  And feel your blood curdle with horror and fright,
That laughter, so shrill, is the sign of a kill
  The Hyena's one joy and delight.

The Stupid Crocodile

A sleepy Croc
  Sat on a rock
    Drowsing in the sun.
      He'd caught a lot of fish that day
        And eaten every one.
          The clouds came out
            to hide the sun,
              The rain came pouring down.
              That silly Croc
              stayed on the rock
              For fear the fish would drown.

Lost Property

An Elephant once lost his trunk
 And found himself completely sunk
He couldn't feed, he couldn't sneeze
 He couldn't pull down any trees,
A lovely bath of muddy water
 Didn't work the way it oughter.
No one knew quite what to say,
 Auntie Ellie knelt to pray.
Mum and Dad and babies all
 Didn't like the sight at all.

Gradually his dreadful fate
Grew too much to contemplate
 And, letting out a piercing scream,
 He woke, to find it was a dream.

Home at Last

A Frog and a Toad
  took a walk down the road.
The Frog said; 'It's dangerous here
  There are horrid contraptions
With wheel like adaptions,
  Of these I have reason to fear.'

    The Toad said: 'I think
  We'll go back to the drink
    To the water of which we are fond.'
So they both hopped along
  For their legs were so strong
And now they are safe in the pond.

Pussycat Paganini

Hey diddle diddle!
The Cat played the fiddle
But what I should like to know
Is: 'How did he manage those pegs that you twiddle
and how did he hold the bow?
The fiddle's an awkward thing to play
And learning it can be hell,
But, in the old rhyme, they never say
If the Cat played the fiddle *well!*

The Lion King

The Lion is a handsome beast
   But he's terribly lazy, to say the least,
His wives do hunting and rear the kids
   And everything else their master bids.

He's a tolerant father, so they say,
   And sometimes will wake for some lazy play
But, if cubs get cheeky, he lets out a roar:–
   'I'm the King of all beasts and I've told you before!'

And then, just to show his unquestioned might,
   He will slowly climb to a suitable height
And pose on a rock, for all to see
   His feline beauty and majesty.

The Exemplary Cheetah

The Cheetah is fleeter than all of his foes
   And yet he'll continually lie down and doze:
He spends all the afternoon under a tree
   In pure relaxation, with the family.

The Sprinter, each winter, goes on with his training,
   He mustn't relax, as he's always explaining.
He measures each metre and, unlike the Cheetah,
   He keeps on the go if it's snowing or raining.

Relaxing's not taxing yet some think it so
   And yet they continually keep on the go.
If man took a lesson from animal life
   He'd save so much worry and trouble and strife.

Cooking Instructions

Four and Twenty Blackbirds
  All began to sing
    When they were baked in a pie
      for the King.
Four and Twenty Blackbirds
  Surely should have died
    If, in the oven,
      They were baked or fried.

'How could this have happened
  Will you tell me please?
Were they first preserved
  In the fridge or the freeze?'

(From an old nursery rhyme.)

Jeremy Fisher

Jeremy Fisher went out for a spree.
   Jeremy Fisher was smart as can be,
He looked at his calendar, tore off the date,
   Said: 'I must go fishing before it's too late'
So he got out his tackle, with worms for a bait,
   He paddled along on a fine lily leaf
'But here' I must tell you 'his journey was brief'
   The lily leaf sank and he leapt for the shore
and declared he'd not travel that way any more
   He made himself comfy and chose a nice place
'And now' he declared 'I have plenty of space
   My tackle, my picnic of sandwiches too.

I've chosen some nice ones, too good to be true!'
   He cast for a long time, but never a bite
He said: 'this is really a terrible plight'
   He munched all his sandwiches, lettuce and fish
'That makes me feel better, my favourite dish.'
   And, just as the light was beginning to fade
He landed a whopper: *'I've done it'* he said.
   He packed up his tackle and took home his fish
And feasted that night on his succulent dish.
   'I've had a good time' Mr Jeremy said,
So he went for a swim and then hopped into bed.

(Apologies to Beatrix Potter)

Mrs Tiggywinkle

Mrs Tiggywinkle was short and rather fat.
   Mrs Tiggywinkle had prickles through her hat
Mrs T. adopted a little tiny mouse
   And they both lived together in a cosy little house.

She washed and ironed and cooked fine food
   And all she did was really good.
She asked some fieldmice in to tea
   And worked in canteens all for free.

   Her neighbours often came to call
     A little lady, loved by all.
   One day the mayor of Wonderland
     Took Mrs Tiggy by the hand.

Bestowed on her a crock of gold
   'Tis yours, my dear, to have and hold.
I've heard how much the wood folk praise
   your kindness and your winning ways.

     (Apologies to Beatrix Potter)

The Lazy Sow

Have you heard of Mother Pig,
   whose ten small piglets grew too big?
When, down the road, in letters clear,
   It said PLEASE PUT YOUR LITTER HERE.
'How lovely,' said the lazy sow,
   'I'll put them in that sack right now.
Perhaps I'll keep just two or three
   to stay and warm the sty for me ... '

That night she stretched in languid grace
   Indulging in the roomy space
But on the next day, sad to say,
   the dust cart took the sack away
And she was in a dreadful state
   about her seven piglets' fate.

The dustman drove right to the dump
   and put the sack down with a bump.
Four small piglets tumbled out
   'Now what can this be all about?'
And then there fell three piglets more
   who all lay squealing on the floor.
The dustman said, 'What have we here?
   They must have all been lost, I fear;
I'll take them all back home right now!'

'Oh, thank you!' said the lazy sow.
'I've learnt my lesson, that's for sure.
I won't be selfish any more!'

Time for a Change

God created Animals
  And said: 'My work is done?'
But now I wish he'd change his mind
  It really would be fun.

    I'd like to see a Chimpanzee
      as tiny as a Bumble bee
    And it would give me such a laugh
      to own a fifteen-inch Giraffe.

    If Zebra's stripes
      were changed to spots
        of pink and yellow polka dots,
    Whilst Pigs had wings and flew on high
      And Doves cooed gently from the sty.

    If Dogs said: 'Meow' and Cats 'Bow-wow'
      And man went riding on a Cow
  Whilst Camels grazed the Farmer's lands
    And hump-backed Sheep
      traversed the sands.

I'd keep some Monkeys in the bath
  With Hippos dozing on the hearth.
I'd have a small-sized Kangaroo
  Whose leap was just an inch or two.

I'd take a Tiger for a walk
   And teach a Crocodile to talk
      Whilst Elephants could learn to dance
         If someone gave them half a chance.

    There's such a lot, you must agree,
      I'd do, if it were up to me.